Pushing and Pulling

by Natalie Hyde

Crabtree Publishing Company

www.crabtreebooks.com

Motion Close-Up

Author
Natalie Hyde

Publishing plan research and development
Reagan Miller

Editor
Reagan Miller

Proofreader
Kathy Middleton

Notes for adults
Reagan Miller

Design
'Katherine Berti

Photo research
Katherine Berti
Reagan Miller

Prepress technicians and production coordinators
Katherine Berti
Ken Wright

Print coordinator
Margaret Amy Salter

Photographs
iStockphoto: page 22 (right); Lokibaho: page 5
Thinkstock: pages 8, 18, 21, 22 (left), 24 (force and direction)
Other images by Shutterstock

Library and Archives Canada Cataloguing in Publication

Hyde, Natalie, 1963-, author
        Pushing and pulling / Natalie Hyde.

(Motion close-up)
Includes index.
Issued in print and electronic formats.
ISBN 978-0-7787-0529-1 (bound).--ISBN 978-0-7787-0533-8 (pbk.).--
ISBN 978-1-4271-9018-5 (html).--ISBN 978-1-4271-9022-2 (pdf)

        1. Force and energy--Juvenile literature. 2. Power (Mechanics)--
Juvenile literature. 3. Motion--Juvenile literature. I. Title.

QC73.4.H93 2014   j531'.6   C2014-900796-5
                                          C2014-900797-3

Library of Congress Cataloging-in-Publication Data

CIP available at the Library of Congress

Crabtree Publishing Company

Printed in Canada/032014/BF20140212

www.crabtreebooks.com   1-800-387-7650

Published in Canada
Crabtree Publishing
616 Welland Ave.
St. Catharines, Ontario
L2M 5V6

Published in the United States
Crabtree Publishing
PMB 59051
350 Fifth Avenue, 59th Floor
New York, New York 10118

Published in the United Kingdom
Crabtree Publishing
Maritime House
Basin Road North, Hove
BN41 1WR

Published in Australia
Crabtree Publishing
3 Charles Street
Coburg North
VIC 3058

Contents

What is motion?

Motion is movement. When something moves, it is in motion. There are things moving around you everywhere you look. Planes fly through the air. Water flows down a stream. People dance.

There are many kinds of motion. Objects can spin, slide, jump, bounce, rock, and swing.

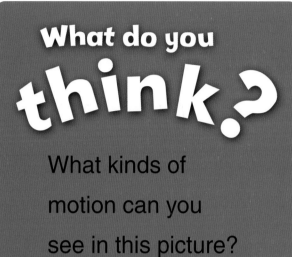

What do you think?

What kinds of motion can you see in this picture?

What is a force?

Things cannot move on their own.

It takes a **force** to make things move.

A force is a push or a pull

that creates motion.

This wagon will not

move without a force.

We cannot see a force. We can only see it work. Wind pushes the water on top of a lake. We cannot see the wind but we can see the waves it makes.

Is it a push or a pull?

A push and a pull are two kinds of forces. A push and a pull are opposites. A push moves something away from you. You push a ball when you throw it. A pull moves something closer to you. You pull on your socks when you get dressed.

What do you think?

Is this girl using a push or pull to move the wagon? How do you know?

Parts for pushing

You push things using different parts of your body. You use your hands to push a friend on a swing. You push your feet against the ground when you walk, run, or jump.

Things can push us, too. A strong wind pushing against you makes it harder to walk. A strong wave can push you over at the beach.

11

Is it still a push?

Any action that moves an object away from you is a push. Kicking, blowing, and sliding are pushing actions. You kick a soccer ball with your foot to push it down the field. You push air out of your mouth to blow out candles.

What do you think?

Is this girl using a push or a pull to hit the tennis ball? How do you know?

Give it a pull!

You use a pulling force everyday. You pull down on a string to open the window blinds. You pull up on weeds when you help in the garden.

Things pull on us, too. **Gravity** is a force that pulls things toward the ground. No matter how high you jump, gravity will always pull you back down to the ground.

Lift—a push or a pull?

Lifting something brings it closer to you. It is a pulling force. You lift a glass to your mouth to drink. You lift a weight when you exercise.

This boy used a pulling force to lift the puppy. What force will he use to put the puppy back down on the ground? How do you know?

Changing direction

A push or a pull can change the **direction** of a moving object. Hitting a volleyball that is moving toward you makes the ball go in another direction. Your hit creates a push that changes the direction of the ball.

This boy changes the direction the yoyo is moving by pulling up on the string.

The amount of force

A big push or pull creates more force than a small push or pull. You need to use a big push to move a heavy object, like a car. You only need to use a small push to move something that is light, like a feather.

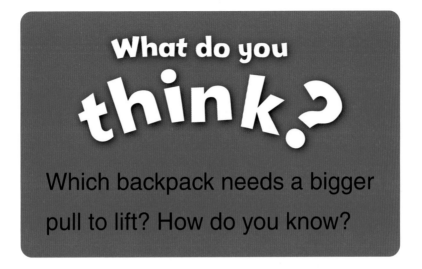

What do you think?

Which backpack needs a bigger pull to lift? How do you know?

Name that force!

Use what you have learned about pushing and pulling to answer these questions.

1. Do you use a push or a pull to zip up your coat?

2. Do you use a push or a pull to spin the merry-go-round?

3. Do you use a push or a pull to climb a rope?

4. Do you use a push or a pull to blow bubbles?

5. Do you use a push or a pull to pick an apple from a tree?

You did a great job!
You are a pushing
and pulling pro!

Words to know and Index

direction

force

gravity

motion

Notes for adults and an activity

This activity encourages collaborative learning and reinforces the child's ability to identify pushing and pulling forces.

Materials: Various objects that use pushes and pulls: wind-up toy, dominoes, balloon, thread spool, roll of tape, spring, windmill, bubble wand, measuring tape, etc.

1. Divide children into small groups. Provide each group with a selection of objects from the materials list above. Review your rules for sharing materials before proceeding.

2. Explain that children are going to be "Force Detectives." Their job is to work as a group to:
a) Identify the force used to move each object (push or pull).
b) Describe the motion created by the force.

3. Have each child create a three-column chart (shown below) in their science journal or prepare a handout prior to the lesson.
Children will use the chart to record their observations. Fill in one example on the chart as a class to ensure children understand format.

Force Detectives		
Object	Force	How object moves
windmill	push	The windmill spins.

4. Each group can present their chart to the class. Encourage meaningful discussion by posing questions such as: What do you think would happen if...? How do you know...?

Learning more

Books

Amazing Forces and Movement by Sally Hewitt, Crabtree Publishing Company, 2007.

Forces: Pushes And Pulls by Angela Royston, Rosen Publishing, 2012.

Websites

This website includes an engaging activity that tests different pushes and pulls on a rolling object. www.bbc.co.uk/schools/scienceclips/ages/5–6/pushes–pulls.shtml

Hubpages talks about force and how it can change the direction of an object.
http://joanca.hubpages.com/hub/Learn-About-Motion-and-Force-for-Kids